GRANDEUR OF INDIA

HARSHITHA NADIKUDA

ISBN 979-888629301-2

Contents

Contents

Contents

Preface

The book "Grandeur of India" is about the magnificence of our nation. It demonstrates about the glory which constructs the beauty of India. The main purpose of this book is to make the people around aware about the India, in an interesting way.

Now-a-days, students are indulged in their academics. So, there is a lack of knowledge about our motherland. Though we study about our nation we feel bored sometimes. So, this book injects information about India in a fascinating manner. Irrespective of age, people can enjoy as well as realize the importance of India.

Preface

Acknowledgements

I feel a deep sense of gratitude to Almighty for guiding me in my every move.

My kind regards to my family, mentors and friends, who genuinely encouraged, supported and inspired me.

Prologue

It was Sunday, children gathered at a place. All were confused to decide an activity to be done on their holiday.

Suddenly, a child came up with an idea and said, “lets grasp the knowledge about the gleam of our motherland.” Another one replied, “Yeah! That’s a fantastic idea.” And they have been to a wise woman.

“Hello aunt! We came to see you for seeking awareness about our nation in an engrossing manner” uttered those children. As she was mesmerized by their keen interest and love towards our nation, she started describing about India poetically…

India - A Subcontinent

Our motherland India is the 7th largest country, in the world. It has a vast land with many diversity features. It is also known as sub-continent as it possess features of a

continent too.

The geography of India is so interesting. We can come across the natural beauty all over the India.

Climatic conditions, topographical features vary and have a

unique features in each region within our nation.

The mountains, hills, rivers, seas, plateaus, plains, forests, islands etc are the dazzling beauty of India.

Soothing nature and pleasant climate brings solace. Natural wealth is a base for civilization. And helps in progressive development of the country.

1. THE HIMALAYAS

The Himalayas were formed, and brought beauty to our nation,
Due to the tectonic plate motion,
It's the third largest deposit of ice and snow,
Which were formed many billion years ago.
The mount Everest,
Named after a British surveyor George Everest,
Not only, the Himalayas highest peak,
But also world's highest pinnacle.
The Indus, the Ganga, the Brahmaputra etc rivers rises from the Himalayas,
Becomes a water source, irrigation needs it meets,
By which the agricultural lands get wet,
Helps in yield production, in return to farmers sweat.
Though Himalayas are natural non-living thing,
It is a beauty spot in every spring;
There is much to speak, about its history,
And mistry,
But the words fall short, unfortunately.

2. THE RIVER SYSTEM

The rivers of India,
Passes via,
Various divisions called tributaries,
And finally flows into the seas.
Indus, Ganga, Brahmaputra rises from Himalayas at north,
Known as Himalayan rivers henceforth,
Forms a V-shaped valley.
The peninsula watercourses,
Fed by the rain source,
Mahanadi, Godavari, Krishna, Cauvery, Narmada, Tapi,
Makes people happy,
As it's the water source for southern states;
Who forms a U-shaped valley.
The river system,
Provides livelihood, as it is a solemn.
I'm assure of a thing,
The rhythm that rivers sing,
Will vanish our tension,
When we glance at their colourful pebbles collection.

3. THE GREAT INDIAN DESERT

The Thar Desert,
World's 17th largest one,
And also world's 9th largest subtropical desert,
Situated at north-western India.
It is an infertile soil's land,
With low rain;
So, now don't misunderstand,
It as a waste terrain.
Sweltering hot in the day,
Freezing in the night,
The ship of the desert - camel, walking through its way,
Is indeed, a heart-warmingly beautiful sight.

4. THE WOODLANDS OF INDIA

Forest, the major environmental resource,
Which is a source of means for many.
Sundarbans of West Bengal,
Gir forest of Gujarat,
Sacred Grove of Meghalaya,
Namdapha National park of Arunachal Pradesh,
Jim Corbett National park of Uttarakhand,
Bandipur National Park of Karnataka,
Nilgiri Biosphere Reserve of Tamil Nadu,
Keibul lamjao National park of Manipur,
Nandalur Reserve forest of south-west Chennai,
Kanha National park of Madhya Pradesh, etc,
Are the amazing forests situated in India.
India, a forest land country,
Who is one of the ten forest rich countries,
Which covers 21.67% of nation's land,
As per the estimates of 2019.
Forest, the habitat of wildlife,
Which has been degraded,
Since modernization came into force,
It's a serious concern,
Should be considered as a hot potato.

Greenary brings pleasure,
It can be brought through afforestation,
Get inspired by the environmentalists,
And contribute yourself to save our nature's beauty.

5. THE NORTHERN PLAIN

The Northern plain,
Formed by three rivers interplay,
Indus, Ganga and Brahmaputra along with their tributaries are the main,
To make the soil fertile in their way.
Alluvial soil has the domain,
Where fertile soil array,
To make the land a fertile plain,
Henceforth, a way to intensive agriculture it lays.
Though it is a plain,
Diverse relief features it contains.

6. THE PENINSULAR PLATEAU

A table land,
Composed of the old crystalline, igneous and metamorphic rocks,
Is known as the peninsular plateau,
Formed due to
Breaking and drifting of Godwana land.
It is an oldest landmass,
Which is a volcanic origin,
Surrounded by broad, shallow valleys and hills too,
With a distinct features,
Covered by black soil area,
Also known as Deccan Trap.
They extend from Gujarat to Delhi,
In a southwest-northeast direction.
Aravalli hills are the highly eroded hills,
Which are broken hills,
Lies on the western and northwestern margins
Of peninsular plateau.
The peninsular tableland consists of two broad divisions,
Namely,
The Central Highlands,
And the Deccan Plateau.

7. THE CENTRAL HIGHLANDS

Central Highlands, also known as Malwa plateau,
Which are wider in west but narrower in east in view,
The further eastward extension marks although,
It is known as Chotanagpur plateau,
Formed 60+ years ago.

8. THE DECCAN PLATEAU

A triangular landmass,
Which lies to the South of Tropic of Cancer,
Known as Deccan Plateau.
This area is subdivided into two major geologic-physiographic regions,
An igneous rock plateau with fertile black soil,
And a gneiss peneplain with infertile red soil.
This tableland is rich in minerals,
Which is interrupted by several hills.

Anaimudi Peak,
Their highest summit,
Located in Kerala.
Deccan plateau is higher in the west,
And gently slops eastwards,
Where Western Ghats and Eastern Ghats
Mark western and eastern edges
of the Deccan plateau.

9. EASTERN GHATS

Eastern Ghats stretch from
Mahanadi valley to Nilgiris in South.
They're discontinuous and irregular,
Dissected by rivers
Draining into Bay of Bengal.
They're lower in height,
Whose highest summit is Jindhagada Peak(1,690).

10. WESTERN GHATS

Western Ghats,
Situated parallel to western coast,
Higher than Eastern Ghats,
Stretch from Mahanadi valley,
To Nilgiris in South,
For they are continuous.
Height of ghats
Progressively increase from north to south,
Where the highest pinnacles,
The Annai Mudi (2,695m),
Followed by Doda Betta(2,637m),
Are located on them.

11. COASTAL PLAINS

The Peninsular Plateau,
Flanked by stretch of narrow costal strips,
Moving along the Arabian sea on the West,
And Bay of Bengal on the East.
The western coast,
Which is a narrower plain,
Sandwiched between Western Ghats,
And the Arabian sea.
The northern part of western coast is known as the Konkan,
While the central part is the Kannal plain
And finally the southern stretch is the Malabar coast.
The Eastern plain along the Bay of Bengal,
Which are wide and level,
Situated between eastern ghats and Bay of Bengal,
Where the prominent rivers flows,
By forming an extensive delta.
The northern part of this plain
Named as Northern Circar,
While southern part is the Coromandel coast.
The Lake Chilka,
The largest salt water lake in India,
Lies in Odisha,
To the South of Mahanadi delta,

An important feature along.

12. THE ISLANDS

Island,
Water surroundes,
All the four sides of land;
Lies on India's either side,
Two groups.
The two groups, namely
Andaman and Nicobar Islands,
Lakshadweep Islands.

13. ANDAMAN AND NICOBAR ISLANDS

Group of islands
Located in Bay of Bengal
Extending from north to south,
Known as Andaman and Nicobar Islands.
They're bigger in size,
Numerous and scattered.
Great strategic importance,
The country possess,
As they are so.
Great diversity of flora and fauna,
Assemble the beauty,
Not only for this groups,
But also to the India.
With equator close to them,
They experience equatorial climate,
Covered by thick forests.

14. LAKSHADWEEP ISLANDS

A small area of 32sq.km
Named as the Lakshadweep Islands.
In the year 1973.

Lies close to Malabar coast of Kerala,
Composed of small coral land,
Which is rich in flora and fauna;
Whose administrative headquarters is,
The Kavaratti island.

15. INDIAN STATES AND UNION TERRITORIES

Union India,
Administered by the honorable President,
And ruled by righteous Prime Minister;
Has twenty eight states,
Ruled by Cheif Minister,
And governer acts as head of executive.
While, President of India administrates Union Territories,
Which are eight.

Each one has a capital,
A city that encompasses government's offices and meetings.

16. OUR TRADITION AND CULTURE

India, considered as birth place of some world's major religions
Buddhism, Hinduism and Sikhism.
Also it the place
Where numerous religion people live,
Mostly, Muslim and Christianity have worked their way into population.
People manifest love and affection for each other,
Inspite of different religions;
Our nation is rich in culture and heritage,
Where people tend to celebrate every festival,
Because everyone is treated as a family member,
And will be uttered by a relation.

17. FESTIVALS

Indian festivals,
Classified into two types,
National festivals
And regional festivals,
Which are overall 36.
National festivals,
Celebrated all over the nation,
Independence day, Republic day, Gandhi Jayanti, Children's day, Teacher's day etc
Traditional festivals,
Based on state-wise, religion based and community-wise;
People from all paths of our nation,
Coexist harmoniously.
Festivals, an expressive way
To celebrate our glorious traditions,
By which we rejoice special moments,
Helps to keep connection with the roots of culture,
And initially to preserve the roots of our heritage,
Which relieve us from monotomy of life.

18. DRESSING STYLES

People belonging to different regions,
Has their own dressing styles,
Namely, saree, shalwar kameez, lehenga, churidar etc
Worn by female,
And kurta, dhoti, shirts, pants etc,
Worn by male,
Will be knitted by different types of threads,
Dyed with radiant colours,
And are designed attractively.
For they represent the tradition, culture and region of the people.

19. LANGUAGES

The second most populated country,
Which has an extensive range of languages,
1,000 dialects are spoken,
In which, our constitution recognized 22 regional languages,
And acknowledged Hindi as the National language.

20. SPICES

Indian cuisine,
Tasty Always,
As heavy spices and herbs are within.
Indian spices,
Legendaries for medical purposes,
And food preserves etc
Has been used over 1000's of years.

21. INDIAN CUISINE

31 dishes of our nation,
Came into force since generations,
Delicious due to spices association,
And ingredients collection,
Moreover, tenderness towards the family is the foundation,
For mouth-watering dishes preparation.
Every region has a special reputation,
Regarding cuisine's domination,
Who would never poessess less appreciation.

22. ART FORMS

Indian art,
Shall always be treasured in our heart,
Because, about the civilization it imparts
And hence our art forms never departs.
Sumptuous art forms,
Spreads its beauty without any norms.

23. PAINTINGS

Paintings, enchantes our eyes,
Within them beauty lies.
Madhubani painting,
Bihar's prestigious wing,
Designed with fingers, matchsticks with natural pigments, sings,
The charmer of painting.
A tribal art of Maharastra-Gujarat border, Warli art,
Will be loved a lot,
Nature's beauty it plots,
Stealing our hearts.

The Tanjore paintings,
First painted under the Chola regime
From Tanjavur district of Tamil nadu it steams
Known for magnificient embellishments, with gleam
Painting the Hindu gods and goddesses on wooden planks, its main cream.
Odisha and West Bengal art form
A creative art form,
Cloth based scroll painting, splendour of this form,
Which had a high influence in Mughal era, as its a unique form.

And many more....

But words are not co-operating anymore.

24. RANGOLI

An art form
Originated in the Indian subcontinent,
In which patterns are drawn
On the floor
By using lime stone, flower petals and various materials,
Which is an everyday practice in Hindu households,
Designed on the porch,
To give the warmest welcome to the guests.
Rangoli hold a significant role as well,
It is believed that represents happiness, positivity and liveliness,
Also lime stone is capable of preventing insects to enter the house,
Indeed it is a fact.
Designs are being passed from one generation to the next,
Keeping the tradition and art form alive,
As it is a traditional charm therefore.

25. SCULPTURE ART

An oldest art form,
Depicts daily life, documentation of success,
A good deed or for religious purposes;
Natural rocks sculptured by man,
An art mastered by human beings in the olden times,
An immortal art across the world.
To-date, this sculpture art hasn't became an old hat,
It wore different forms made by using various alloys,
Which attracts the tourists,
And hence brings pleasures to the country as well.

26. PERFORMING ARTS

Performing arts has a well-placed status
In the culture and tradition,
And are well known across the world,
As Indian performing arts are aesthetics,
Based on nava rasas.

27. DANCE

Indian Dance,
Dates back to the ancient Indus Valley Civilization,
Which is the premeval expression of transcending barriers of culture,
And is a part of devotional process;
When combined with music and story telling,
It is metamorphised into theatre.
The different dance forms of India,
Offers scintillating experiences to the viewers,
Along with the major dance forms like
Bharatanatyam, Kuchipudi, Mohiniyattam, Kathakali, Odissi and many more.
Both classics and folk dances
Owe their present popularity;
And dance in India
Has an unbroken tradition of over 2000 years,
Whose themes are derived from mythology, legends and classic literature,
Which entertains people as well as pass a moral.

28. MELODIES

Music is one of the archiac unbroken tradition,
And is said that the evolution of Indian music
Goes back to vedas,
Which has been always connected to emotions,
And undoubtedly it is an intangible asset of human being.
Music has been classified as
The Hindustani and the Carnatic,
Who pours life to oral traditions,
To-date various forms of melodies are born,
And henceforth, traditions carries sublime quality of music,
Because music is eternal.

29. INDIAN THEATRE

One of the most ancient forms of theatre
Which features a detailed textual, sculptural and dramatic effects,
Emerged in mid first millennium BC.
Indian Theatre not only entertains,
But also to educates people,
Henceforth, it possess the highest achievement of Sanskrit literature.
Numerous forms of theatre,
With a motive to spread culture,
And to conserve our Indian heritage,
Are praiseworthy for-keeps.
Kathputli, a pupperty show,
About various stories shows,
With the help of puppets
Which is a famous art form of Rajasthan's sets;
An exemplary form of Indian Theatre,
And there are diverse forms of this too.
Past theatre,
Now took a form of cinema.

30. CINEMA

Indian flims,
Immensely popular ones,
Amuses people,
For they has a unique theme and genre.
Movies produced in various languages,
Holds different styles and emotions,
With them culture spreads and as well as wise sayings too.

31. LITERATURE

Literature produced on the Indian subcontinent,
Until 1947 and thereafter,
Refers to the Indian literature;
22 languages are official recognised, therefore.
The earliest works of Indian literature
Were orally transmitted,
And thereafter vedas, epic and many wise sayings
Were penned to bring forth mortality.
Literature arisen myraid scripts inked by the writers,
Which harness the evil,
And passes good to descendants,
Which is a paramount,
For spreading our heritage.

32. BOOKS

Literature has come a long way
From books with different genres and themes,
Lauching every year,
Which are fascinatingly penned by numerous writers.
With so many books releasing
Indian literature is developing by leaps and bounds,
As words are swords of the poet's,
For they use them in different ways,
To convey tenderness as well as to slay.
Various scribbles were written by freedom fighters,
To spread the importance of independence,
And to manifest hateredness towards Britishers.
Indian literature,
Definitely has to receive exaltation,
As their exalt yearn poets sense.
The sense of the books,
Has to be utterly grasped,
As they depict moral,
And illuminates our life.

33. ARCHITECTURE

The architecture of India,
Rooted in its history, culture and religion,
Best known for their contrasting architecture
And historical styles.
They're prosperity of the nation,
Which treasures glorious,
And does wonders when we glance at them,
And it's obvious that in Indian architecture
Benevolence dwells.
Our forerunners beorganed the treasure,
And we too must conserve its charm,
As the art of India is chaste for-keeps.

34. MONUMENTS

116 monuments in 19 states,
Managed by Archeological Survey of India,
Devising the beauty of India.
India, one of the countries
Which own incredible beauty,
Colourful culture and fascinating heritage.
Its grand monuments,
Act as strong pillars of our history,
Which are built by
The stones that brings glory of rulers
And brilliance of artisans
Of ancient India.
By the constant efforts of government,
The Indian heritage sites are protected;
Tourism has flourished rapidly,
Witnessing a rise in number of travellers
From all around the world.
All monuments conquered the beauty,
And presented to the India therefore.
Spendid architecture indeed!

35. THE TAJ MAHAL

White marble mausoleum built,
By Mughal Emperor Shah Jahan
For his wife Mumtaz Mahal.
The Taj Mahal,
A testimony to love,
Which has a bedazzling art work,
Along with sheen of marbles,
Located in Arga,
On the southern bank of river Yamuna.
Thus, an admired master pieces of world's heritage.

36. RED FORT

Historic fort in Delhi,
Was a residential of Mughal emperor,
Commissioned construction on 12th May 1638,
For when dedicated to shift country's capital
From Agra to Delhi.
With plundered artwork and jewels,
It represents the peak of Mughal architecture
Under leadership of Shah Jahan.
That's all about history.
But, it's not the end for its vogue
On red letter day of ours-Independence day
Jawaharlal Nehru rose our tricoloured flag,
And every year prime minister of India does so.

37. HARMANDIR SAHIB (GOLDEN TEMPLE)

Harmandir Sahib,
MeansAbode of God
A Gurudwara located in Amritsar, Punjab.
The Golden temple,
A preeminent spritual site,
And most significant shrine in Sikhism.
An open house of worship,
For all people,
From all walks of life and faiths.
Interior of Darbar Sahib
With God encrusted walls
And featuring a golden chandelier,
A spellbound architecture indeed!

38. THE CHARMINAR

The Charminar,
Constructed by the fifth ruler of Qutb Shahi dynasty,
Mohammad Quli Qutb Shah,
In the year 1591,
Located in Hyderabad, Telangana.

The landmark of Hyderabad,
Also been officially incorporated,
As the Emblem of Telangana,
Which has long history behind.
It was built at the centre of city,
To commemorate the eradication of plageau,
A said story.
Structure made of granite, limestone, mortor and pulverised marble,
Weighing approximately 14,000 tones a piece,
Whose eponymous towers are ornate minarets,
Attached and supported by four grand arches;
Listed as an archeological and architectural treasure
On the official List of Monuments,
Situated at East Bank of Musi River.
The heart of Attraction!

39. AJANTA CAVES AND ELLORA CAVES

The beauty of Ajanta caves,
Lies in their famed paintings and murals,
Located in Aurangabad district of Maharashtra,
Includes finest surviving art of Indian art,
Which mesmerizes tourists with its stonework too,
Who has a large emphasis on teaching and learning,
Where education and worship is under a central direction.
In 1983, Ajanta Caves were listed
As UNESCO World Heritage Site.
While Ellora's wealth
Lies in the caves sculptures and rich architecture,
34 rock monasteries and temple
Dug side by side in a wall of a high basalt cliff,
Are a celebration of 3 major religions -
Hinduism, Buddhism and Jainism.
Monolithic Kailasa Temple,
The signature cave of Ellora,
The largest single excavation in the world,
Attracts numerous visitors;
Not only a single cave,
But also every art form in them,
Are beautiful.

40. THE KANGRA FORT

The Kangra fort,
Built by the Royal Rajput family,
Traces its origins to the ancient Trigarta kingdom,
Mentioned in the Mahabharata epic,
Which is the largest fort in the Himalayas,
And probably the oldest dates fort in India.

41. DILWARA TEMPLE

Group of Svetambara Jain temple,
Located about 2+ kilometres from the Mount Abu settlements,
Rajasthans only hill station,
Named as Dilwara temple.
Built between 11th and 16th centuries,
Forming one of the most famous monuments
In style of Maru Gurjara Architechture,
Well known for their very pure white marble,
And intricate marble carvings.
The prominent piligrimage place for Jains,
Built by Vimal Shah,
A significant general tourist spot.

42. QUTB MINAR

A minarant and victory tower
Forms part of Qutub Complex;
UNESCO World Heritage site located in Delhi,
Which is one of the most visited tourist spots
One of earliest surviving architecture in Indian subcontinent.
Its surface is eloborately decorated
With inscriptions and geometric patterns,
Where the whole part is built
By using different materials, techniques and decorations;
Initially, the minaret is unique historically,
Started spreading its beauty around 1192
By Qutb-ud-din-Aibak,
The first ruler of Delhi Sultanate.
The Qubt Minar,
A symbol of traditional Islamic construction,
And a synthesis of South Asian architecture.

43. RUDRESHWARA SWAMY TEMPLE

Thousand pillars temple,
A historic one,
Located in the town of Hanamakonda, Telangana,
Dedicated to Lord Shiva, Vishnu and Surya.
Other captivating constructions,
Surrounding the Rudreshwara temple,
Namely, Warangal Fort, Kakatiya Kara Thoranam, Ramappa Temple;
Were added to the tentative list of World Heritage sites,
Recognised by UNESCO.
Numerous Hindu Temples,
Were developed under the patronage
Of kings of Kakatiya Dynasty;
1000 pillars temple,
Constructed during 1175-1325CE,
By the order of Rudra Deva,
Which stands out to be a masterpiece
And achieved major heights
In forms of architectural skills,
As it is one of the finest Kakatiya art.
There are richly carved
A thousand pillars,

Perforated screens,
Exquisite icons,
Rock cut elephants,
And monolithic dolerite Nandi,
As components of the temple;
Which is known for its Flawless ivory carving.

44. BRIHADISHVARA TEMPLE

A Hindu Temple,
Dedicated to lord Shiva,
Also known as Rajarajeshwaram,
Located in the south bank of Cauvery River in Tamil Nadu;
Which is one of the largest south Indian temples
And it is an exemplary example tamil architechture.
The Brihadishvara temple,
Constructed by Tamil king Raja Raja Chola 1
Between 1003 and 1010 AD;
Built around a moat,
With granite,
Which consists
Gopura, the main temple, its massive tower, inscriptions, frescoes, sculptures.
The Vimana tower,
Tallest in sourthern India,
Which is above the shrine.
The temple has a massive colonnaded prakara
And one of the largest Shiva lingas in India;
Also framed for the quality of its sculptures,
For being the location that commissioned the brass Nataraja.

45. HAWA MAHAL

Hawa mahal,
Situated in Jaipur,
Built with red and pink sandstone structure,
Built in 1799 by Pratap Singh,
Grandson of Maharaja Sawai Jai Singh,
Who was the founder of Jaipur.
The palace is a five-storied pyramidal shaped monument,
Rises about 15 feet;
Which are like honeycomb,
With small portholes,
Within them 953 miniature windows are present,
Decorated with latticework,
And carved sandstone grills, finials and domes.
Interior of the palace,
Has been designed
With different coloured marbles;
While fountains adorn the centre of the courtyard.
An architectural museum is also housed
In this courtyard,
Spreading its elegance over the nation.

46. THE VICTORIA MEMORIAL

A large marble building in Kolkata,
Built between 1906 and 1921,
Dedicated to the memory of Empress Victoria;
And now it is a museum
Under auspices of the Ministry of Culture,
Lies on the maidan,
Which is one of the famous monuments of Kolkata.
The death of Empress Victoria,
Resulted a thought to Lord Curzon,
To build a memorial for her,
Who then proposed the construction of a grand building
With a museum and a garden.
The memorial was built of white Makrana marble,
And has a design of Indo-Saracenic revivalist style,
With 25 galleries of museum and gardens too.

47. THE SANCHI STUPA

The great Stupa at Sanchi,

A Buddhist complex,

Famous for its stupa on the hilltown at Sanchi town of Madhya Pradesh.

It is one of the oldest stone structure in India,

And an important monument of Indian Architechture,

Originally commissioned by Mauryan emperor Ashoka the great

In 3rd century BCE.

Sanchi stupa is depicted on

The reverse side of the Indian currency note of Rs. 200

Signifies its importance to Indian cultural heritage.

48. MEENAKSHI TEMPLE

Arulmigu Meenakshi Sundareshwarar Temple,
A historic Hindu temple,
Located on the southern bank of Vaigai River of Madurai;
Dedicated to goddess Meenakshi,
A form of Parvati,
And her consort Sundareshwar,
A form of lord Shiva.

More than 2500 years ago,
The temple was built by Pandyan king, Kulashekarar,
In the 6th century,
At the heart of city of Madhurai.

Sculpted pillars,
Are adorned with exquisite murals;
There are 985 richly carved pillars
And each one surpasses the beauty of other.

The chat of hymns,
Cultural events,
Tradition, devotion,
Brings charm to the temple.

Modernity has reached the city,
But not at the cost of its rich culture and heritage.

49. LOTUS TEMPLE

The Lotus temple,
Notable for its flowerlike shape,
Located in New Delhi,
Which is open for all the walks of life,
A forever prominent attraction of the city.
The name of the temple
Derived from its eye-catching construction,
Which is nine sided,
Situated on elevated plinth expanse of landscaped gardens,
With nine pools surrounded by them,
Boarded by the red sandstone walkways,
And the white marble edifice.
This beautiful construction
Comprises of 27 independent marble petals,
Which are clustered into three groups to form nine sides
And three concentric rings.
The first face outward
Forming canopies over the nine entrances,
The second covers the outer hall,
And the innermost ring petals curves inward partially,
Which encloses the central prayer hall,
For which has a surface
Made of white marble from Penteli mountain in Greece.

A floating lotus flower
On the verge of blooming and surrounded by its leaves,
Won numerous architectural awards,
And received a wide range of attention in various venues.

50. RED LETTER DAYS OF INDIA

Indian important days
Educate and spread awareness in different ways,
Reflects on bundle thoughts of hay
And gives a rise to a ray.
Initially, Independence day,
About which there is much to say,
We got our freedom in August 15, 1947 on this day,
Which was earlier exposed to betray.
The republic day,
Celebrated from 26th January 1950 every year on this day,
Constitution took its way,
And came into force which we must obey.
The youth day,
Celebrated on 12th January on Swami Vivekananda's birthday,
Displays Vivekananda's thoughts in array,
By which youth never go astray.
Every year on 21st june we celebrate Yoga day,
With the awareness, yoga would never decay,
Prominently, it kills all our mental preys,
Because is an eminent exercise in all ways.
On 14th November, children's day,
On 5th September, teacher's day,

On 15th October, students day, etc,
The red letter days, on them importance lays,
Promoting our admirable Indian glory in all the ways.

51. INDIAN GLORY

The main components of India,
Are the honour of our motherland.
Nation anthem, (Jana Gana Mana.....)
Written by Rabindranath Tagore,
An extract from the book Geetanjali,
Publicly sang on 27th December 1911 at Calcutta.
National song, (Vande Mataram......)
Composed by Bankimchandra Chatterji,
Which is an ode to motherland,
Extracted from Anandmath,
Adopted by Constituent Assembly of India on 24 January 1950.
Our tri-coloured flag,
Designed by Pingali Venkaya,
Which consists of three colours and a chakra
Where the top band Saffron
Represents the strength and courage,
The middle band white indicates peace and truth,
With Darma Chakra depicted wheel of law,
Which intends to show that there is life in movement and death in stagnation,
And last band is green in colour,
Which shows the fertility, growth and auspiciousness of the

land.
And next, the national emblem,
Which has four lions,
It symbolizes power, courage and confidence,
Stands on a circular abacus,
Girded by four smaller animals;
The bull represents hard work and steadfastness,
Elephant represents strength,
Lion shows bravery,
And the horse, loyalty, speed and energy,
The Dharma Charka below the four lions,
Has 24 spokes which represents 24 hours in a day,
Signifying that the time cannot be bounded
And its passage is inevitable;
The motto Satyameva Jayate
Inscribed below the emblem.
Our national bird - Peacock
National animal - Tiger
National flower - Lotus
National tree - Banyan tree
Are are pride of our nation.

52. INVENTIONS OF INDIA

Indian inventions and discoveries,
Reflects on architecture, astronomy, cartography, mathematics, logic and etc
Indian scholars, persuaded knowledge in various fields,
So as to invent and discover which brings benefits
To make the life of the people comfortable.
Integral parts of administration, communication, computers and programming, architecture, games, genetics and many more...
And mathematics, medicine, mining, science, space etc too,
Were invented and discovered by our Indians.
These great inventions aren't enough to be proud of our country?
They are!

53. FREEDOM FIGHTERS

Today we are breathing air
Which contains freedom,
And the independence is the fruit
Given by our freedom fighters
By sacrificing their lives;
Mahatma Gandhi, Jawaharlal Nehru, Bhagat Singh, Subhash
Chandra Bose and many more...
The corpses of our heroes were buried in soil,
Which degrades by time,
But their good deeds are not;
They are deeply buried in the hearts of Indian people,
For they are for-keeps alive.
Many years of struggle,
Colossal sacrifices,
Resulted a peaceful life for us.
Our freedom fighters are not great,
They are beyond that,
As their desire for making India free country,
And their executions are praiseworthy,
Hence, they are eternal in our hearts.

54. UNSUNG HEROES

Unsung heroes,
Extraordinary personalities,
Who believe in strength
To fight against any deadly obstacle,
But are very rarely known to people.
They lay their life wholeheartedly,
To protect someone,
And takes any risk,
For his people,
But he's not popular.
They're real heroes,
They shall be contented
If their deeds are useful to people,
But never they misspent their time for publicity.
There are many unsung heroes,
And we should be inspired by them,
Furthermore, we must inspire others,
This process would knit the humanity,
And hence our India shall be the greatest kingdom,
With great personalities.

55. SOLDIERS - WARRIORS WHO PROTECTS OUR EMINENCE

Indian soldiers,
Doesn't even care for their lives,
As their main motive is to protect our nation,
They're not only protogonist,
But also the replica of courage,
Who dedicates themselves for the motherland,
And survives in the heart of Indian people,
Forever.

56. RESPLENDENCE OF INDIA

Our country is a combination,
Of various religion population,
But there isn't any discrimination,
As every one are called by a relation.
The country of cultivation,
Are presenting hospitality since generations,
For all, without any separation.
To never come across our culture and heritage degradation
The orientation
Of weeds must take place elimination.
Awareness about education,
Right to any information,
Freedom of participation,
And to select our administration,
Many more builds a great civilization.
Our nation,
Has a great administration,
And has a concentration
Towards peoples' needs in every situation.
Following the applications
Of great personalities with our innovations,
Definitely brings transformation,

If there's a strong determination.
India, a developing nation,
Has a good reputation,
And if we want to see it as a developed nation,
We must be the foundation,
To develop our motherland in every application,
Then definitely India shall reach its destination.
Finally I'm giving my declaration,
The collaboration of Indian beauty with peoples' love,
Shall always possess colossal of appreciation.

57. METRICAL COMPOSITION ON OUR NATION

India is a land of courage, which is a sword,
Who protects people in every chord,
And people of the nation are never ignored.
Freedom fighters have restored,
Independence against discords,
And initially cored,
The oppression, which was forged.
Since years, by the law Indians have been accorded,
And protected in every untoward,
And hence India is adored.

58. MOTHERLAND

India,
Safe land for all,
Associated with
Love, and pours the tenderness of
Mother.

Epilogue

.... The wise woman took a break for a while and said, "My dear children, my chronicle about India is just a drop in the ocean, there is much more to speak about our motherland and hence we must show immense respect towards our motherland."

Then, children yelled "Yes aunt, what a beautiful country ours is!"

And finally they ended up by saying,

"JAI HIND"

Epilogue

[illegible]

Thank you for choosing

"GRANDEUR OF INDIA"

9 798886 293012

Printed by Libri Plureos GmbH in Hamburg,
Germany